*Waste not fresh tears
over old griefs.*

Euripides

Other
Health Communications Books
by Bryan E. Robinson

Work Addiction
Hidden Legacies Of Adult Children.

Soothing Moments
Daily Meditations For Fast-Track Living.

Heal Your Self-Esteem
Recovery From Addictive Thinking.

Stressed Out?
A Guidebook For Taking Care Of Yourself.

Healograms: Series 1

Healograms: Series 2

Overdoing It
How To Slow Down And
Take Care Of Yourself.

HEALOGRAMS

4

HOW TO HAVE A HEALTHY OUTLOOK

Bryan E. Robinson, Ph.D.
Jamey McCullers, R.N.

Health Communications, Inc.
Deerfield Beach, Florida

Publisher: Health Communications, Inc.
         3201 S.W. 15th Street
         Deerfield Beach, FL 33442-8190

Graphic design by Graphic Expressions
Color design by Robert Cannata

How To Heal Old Hurts

People in our lives who arouse strong negative feelings in us hold the key to ancient hurts. They make old wounds bleed. They remind us of a person or situation that hurt us in the past. And we blame them for reminding us.

As Eleanor Roosevelt said, "No one can make us feel inferior without our consent." We have to already feel inferior deep inside, but these are *our* wounds, not theirs. The people who cause us to sizzle are messengers who remind us the wounds are still there. Instead of resenting them, we can look upon them as teachers and ask ourselves, "What is already there inside that they are pointing to?"

These *Healograms* — positive, healthy messages we send to ourselves — help us heal old emotional wounds. They help us to understand the true source of our feelings and to forgive and even thank the messenger in our lives for helping us uncover those buried feelings.

This booklet contains written *Healograms* that can help you heal old hurts from the past that keep erupting like a volcano and interfering with your life today. Reflect on each of the messages and silently apply them to your life. Then become actively involved in the healing process as you write your own *Healograms* in the spaces provided.

How To Have A Healthy Outlook

Healing Old Wounds

Many of us cart around hurtful past experiences that keep our lives from working. When we let unresolved hurts interfere with our lives, we repel others.

We can heal these old wounds by recognizing that the pain is in the past and not confusing it with our lives today.

We heal old wounds by not allowing the past to contaminate

our present. We need not respond in the same dysfunctional ways today as we did yesterday because we are not the same person. We have grown. We live with a fresh clean state and open ourselves to health and happiness. The key to healing old hurts is forgiveness. Forgiving ourselves and others who have hurt us in the past frees us to live joyfully in the present. Once we begin to let go of old feelings and hurts, we begin to heal our wounds and begin to attract people into our lives, rather than push them away.

*W*hen we decide to let go of old feelings and hurts, we begin to heal our wounds and to attract people into our lives, rather than push them away.

Recycling The Past

How many of us are waiting for the ax to fall or are worrying that something terrible might happen, even when there is no good reason? Fear of catastrophe is a habit that comes from past trauma. Because our past experience of life consisted of fear and abuse, we believe that's all there is to life. So we recycle the past in our minds and worry that the worst will continue to happen. The past and future become one and we miss the present altogether.

Once we feel our feelings and know that the past is over and gone, we don't have to keep digging it up and recreating it.

We can start fresh and live in the now by letting go of old fears that no longer serve us. We can remind ourselves that we deserve better treatment and expect the best life has to offer.

*O*nce we feel our feelings and know that the past is over and gone, we don't have to keep digging it up and recreating it unless we choose to do so.

Learning To Say No

Why do so many of us spread ourselves too thin and then end up anxious, mad and exhausted? Because it is hard to say no. We worry that people won't like us if we deny them their request. We feel we're not worthy if we cannot meet every demand. We may even go so far as to think that God sent this person and to deny them is to deny God's will.

Our minds can think up any excuse to keep us from taking care of ourselves. Everytime we say yes when we mean no, we do ourselves and the requester an injustice. As long as we are compelled to say yes, we build bars on our self-imposed prison of obligation and guilt. We feel resentful and burnt out.

What makes us feel we must be all things to all people? We can never freely say yes until we can genuinely say no when the request is too much.

We can never freely say yes until we can genuinely say no when we are already overloaded.

Disciplining Our Minds

Sometimes our minds get away with murder. We put ourselves down, call ourselves names and use shame-based thinking. We repeat in our heads all the messages we heard as children. But we don't have to continue to abuse ourselves with the false thoughts from our childhoods.

First, we should become aware of the thoughts with which we

abuse ourselves. We start to listen to the ugly names we call ourselves and the negative statements we allow to pile up inside of us. Next we refuse to accept the untruths by standing up to the negative self-talk. And then we replace the ugly thoughts with more accurate positive thoughts.

As we begin to flood ourselves with loving thoughts, we are able to rise above our former distorted view of the world. As we discipline our minds, they become clearer and more rational and we feel more in charge.

When we discipline our minds by taking charge of our thoughts, they become clearer and more rational and we feel more in charge, more grown-up.

5

Sharing Our Feelings

It can be lonely and frightening when others don't understand what it's like to be overcome with emotional pain or grief. We may feel angry that others don't detect that we're having problems, offer a sympathetic ear or react in the ways we expect. After all, we've given them enough hints that we're hurting.

Many of us beat around the bush instead of directly sharing our feelings. We cannot expect loved ones to be mind readers. We cannot expect them to feel *exactly* the way we do or to say and do something that would solve our problem for us. Once we openly share our hurt and sorrow without expectation, the most we can hope for is that our loved ones will listen and be supportive. What greater gift of love?

*O*nce we openly share our feelings with those we trust, the most we can hope for is that they will listen and be supportive, but we can never expect them to solve our problems for us.

6

Replacing Fear
With Love

Fears seem to be a part of everyone's life. Increases in crime, wars, global warming and famine, with newscasts giving detailed accounts of these events, further increase our fears. We start to fear others if we didn't already and we begin shutting down our emotions. Fear will even invade our sleep in the form of dreams. How is it possible to live in a world

without such constant bombard-
ment from our fears?

This is where spiritual develop-
ment and practice is so necessary.
Developing that inward strength
can be a comfort. We replace the
fears that we learned in the physical domain with the love that we
carry from our spiritual domain,
which expresses our true nature
as human beings. This replace-
ment helps us walk through our
daily fears without taking them
inside where they can paralyze us.

Replacing the fears that we learned in the physical domain with the love that expresses our true nature helps us to walk through scary situations.

7

Making Healthy Choices

One of the greatest anxiety relievers is knowing that we do not have to leave our lives to chance. Each of us is making choices every second of our lives. Even when we refuse to make a decision, we have made a choice.

As we learn to take charge of our lives, we no longer let situations paralyze us. We do not let other people or circumstances make decisions for us. We see that it is up to us to make healthy choices and we begin to seek solutions instead of waiting for them to fall in our lap.

As we choose to focus on joy and gratitude instead of lack and discontent, our lives are filled with happiness and satisfaction. We learn to recognize and avoid things in our lives that cause stress and learn to replace them with serenity. We learn that we do have choices in our lives and that it is up to us to maintain that healthy focus.

We can recognize and avoid things in our lives that cause stress and maintain a healthy focus through balance.

8

Encouraging Ourselves

There are days when we find ourselves behaving in ways that are contrary to all the personal growth we have made. Perhaps we snap at a friend, criticize a co-worker or laugh at someone who is overweight. It's as if our mind is on automatic pilot with the past and we catch ourselves in the middle of old actions before we realize it. We become discouraged and shame ourselves for falling into old behavior patterns.

Doubts and discomforts with old behaviors are healthy signs of progress. It shows that we can recognize and prefer better ways of living from the past. We have learned to spot old habits as they try to sneak back into our lives. The key is to remember that our aim is personal progress, not personal perfections. Instead of shaming, we can forgive ourselves and look at how far we have come. We can replace discouragement with encouragement.

We can encourage ourselves by looking at how far we have come, instead of how far we have to go and by spotting unhealthy habits when they try to sneak back into our lives.

Breaking And Developing Habits

Our habits slowly mount up over time to make us who we are. Some are positive, some negative. Just as streams eventually turn into rivers and rivers make up the seas, so too our habits gradually add up. We can ask ourselves, "Are our habits taking us into rough waters and wild rapids? Or are they carrying us into calm and serene seas?"

Habits are made and they can be broken. Each opportunity we have to break a bad habit puts us further down our healing path. Broken habits also slowly build to transform us into the type of person we want to be. Personal progress begins with the breaking of just one unhealthy habit that when multiplied yields a total healthy person. We can ask ourselves which habits in our lives need breaking and which need developing.

The breaking of just one unhealthy habit at a time, when multiplied, adds up to a total healthy person. The difficult part sometimes is knowing which habits need breaking and which need developing.

Developing Healthy Outlooks

Our minds often resist the things we need to know. This can happen when we hear a lecture, read a passage or listen to a friend say something that conflicts with our beliefs about ourselves and the world. People who feel unworthy, for example, might screen conversations so that they ignore positive comments and compliments and collect only negative affirmations and put-downs — all of which match how they view themselves.

How can we learn to see and hear what we have been resisting? First we become aware of our mind's resistance and then remove the blocks. We learn to see and hear more of life around us and welcome the new and unfamiliar. We create change by doing things differently, breaking routines, spending time with new friends and in new situations. We look at the whole picture of our lives, not just a piece of it.

We can begin to develop healthy outlooks by looking at the whole picture of our lives, not just one piece of it and by opening ourselves to change, new people, unfamiliar situations and different ways of living.

Trusting

Trusting another person is hard when we have been betrayed in the past. Perhaps a close friend let us down or a loved one rejected or abandoned us. We anticipate the same thing happening again and become suspicious of people's intentions. We build walls to protect ourselves and keep others away. This seems to be a lonely way to lead our lives — never getting close to another human being — never letting anyone see who we really are.

It is important to remember that fear is the roadblock to trust. Once we identify and face the fear, we can begin to trust in others again. It all begins with our own trust in ourselves, knowing that we can manage our lives no matter what the situation. The more we trust in our own ability, the more we are able to open up and trust others. We can begin to trust ourselves more and fear ourselves less, and let our hearts guide the way.

46

Trusting others begins with trusting ourselves by knowing that we can manage our lives no matter what the situation.

13

Learning To Have Faith

Faith is what keeps us going when things around us seem to be falling apart. Faith is not a belief but an attitude that is developed and nurtured. As we develop faith, we undergo an attitude change by accepting everything in life as it is without trying to figure it out. On faith Anthony De Mello said, "Nothing has changed but my attitude; everything has changed."

Faith requires us to take risks. As long as doubt ushers our thoughts, there is no need for faith. Doubt furnishes us with fuel to keep us from taking the risks necessary for personal growth. Recognizing doubtful thoughts for what they are — old tapes playing from the past — gives us the power to overcome them. We can extinguish the fire of doubt by changing our attitudes and replacing mistrust with faith.

Recognizing doubtful thoughts for what they are — old tapes playing from the past — gives us the faith that we can overcome them and the power to do so.

14

Expressing Grief

Everyone has to face some grief in life. The act of grieving is feeling the inner hurt and pain so fully (and fully is the key word) that it will melt away. Grieving includes crying out our pain, pounding our feelings out on a pillow, sharing them with a friend or counselor, writing them out on paper or talking them onto a tape recorder.

It is important to remember that we are never alone in our grief because grief is universal. Expressing it soothes and heals us. When we share our grief, we cut it in half because we start to empty it. Each time we share or express our pain, we feel less heavy and burdened. Once we have started the process of grieving our hurt, the healing begins and we can refill the empty space with joy and hope for today.

Grieving soothes and heals by cutting our pain in half and allowing us to refill the empty space with joy and hope.

Burying The Hatchet

Sydney Harris once wrote, "There's no point in burying a hatchet if you're going to put up a marker on the site." Sometimes we pretend to forgive but continue to carry old resentments and self-pity. When we harbor anger and resentment, we literally turn them inward upon ourselves where they can harm us emotionally and physically. Carrying a grudge keeps us stuck in past defeat.

We set ourselves free by releasing destructive feelings and forgiving ourselves and the wrong-doers. Turning our anger into love and forgiveness unblocks our spiritual path. We can begin to bury the hatchet by taking a personal inventory of old feelings and releasing the ones that we are still clutching. Once we bury the hatchet completely, we set ourselves free.

We can begin to bury the hatchet by taking an inventory of old feelings, releasing the ones we still clutch and setting ourselves free once and for all.